BERYL COOK'S
LONDON

BERYL COOK'S
LONDON

JOHN MURRAY

_____

GALLERY FIVE

© Beryl Cook 1988

First published 1988
by John Murray (Publishers) Ltd
50 Albemarle Street, London W1X 4BD
and Gallery Five Ltd, 121 King Street, London W6 9JG

British Library Cataloguing in Publication Data
Cook, Beryl
Beryl Cook's London.
1. English paintings. Cook, Beryl.
Illustrations
I. Title
759.2
ISBN 0-7195-4532-3

Printed in Italy
New Interlitho SpA., Milan

PREFACE

Sometimes we go to London on business affairs, sometimes we go to see friends. Quite often the two overlap, and we're attending to business whilst chatting to friends. Whatever the reason we know that we are going to enjoy ourselves, and will dine at least once at Langan's Brasserie. Many of the things I see and like I can paint as soon as I get home, others spend a long time – sometimes years – in my mind before I find a satisfactory way of dealing with them. You might notice that there are rather a lot of people and very little background in these pictures. I frankly admit that my greatest pleasure is in what people are doing rather than where we are, and they certainly do it in style in London.

THE FAN SHUFFLE

I like the journeys between Plymouth and London
on the train, even without thc toasted bacon
sandwiches that used to be served. There is the first
rush on board to get a good seat, the stacking of the
luggage, and finally we settle down to the coffee
bought with foresight from the station bar so we
don't have to wait for the buffet car to open. Seats
have been reserved with newspapers and briefcases
in some sections for the card schools, dedicated
players sometimes drawing an audience. The
clicking and shuffling of cards beside us on the way
to London caused this picture to be painted. The
man I used as a model was, however, on a plane
journey, and I consider he saved me from a heart
attack. The pilot announced, just before landing,
that we should have to go round again. Overcome
with terror, I looked around at my companions for
what I thought would be the last time, to find that
this man had calmly undone his safety belt and was
busy once more vigorously shuffling and laying out
cards – as he had been for the past six hours.
Obviously *his* last moment hadn't arrived so
neither had mine, and now he shuffles cards
forever on a train.

PADDINGTON STATION

I know more about Paddington than any other station in London. Years ago I travelled there daily from Reading and remember the time when there were cosy coal fires in the Buffet. There is some rearrangement of the station seating, to enable me to get in all the various activities of people starting and finishing their journeys. Or just sitting and waiting, sometimes impatiently I expect: but not on my part for there is always so much to watch. A long wait in a taxi queue was once transformed by a man who appeared from nowhere and, taking charge, ushered us in turn into the arriving taxis with a good-natured commentary composed entirely of the foulest swear-words.

He was eventually removed.

TAXI

And talking of taxis, here is one, chock-full with some colourful characters I thought the driver might like to carry. As there always seem to be massive building operations going on in London, and one of the biggest is right beside where we stay, I've used it as a background. I have trouble depicting highlights (paving stones as well, judging from the tiny size of these) so this is an old taxi that has seen better days instead of a nice bright and shiny one.

ALBEMARLE STREET

In Albemarle Street there are several small cafés
with seats outside, one of them used by taxi drivers
for their morning coffee. We often stop there for
sustenance ourselves, and one day, swinging down
the street, came this lady with her three little dogs.
She was tastefully dressed with brolly to match and
passed us twice so she was evidently making a
circular tour. But no more sitting about in cafés,
time to go further down the street to The Publishers.

B.Cook

THE CORSELETTE

This is what I was hoping to see when we arrived at John Murray's, but no luck. It seems that the only way for a scene like this to materialise is for me to attend a book-launching party dressed in the dainty garment myself. For some years I've kept a small advertisement showing me how to control my bulges with a glistening, gleaming corselette. This fascinated me so much that after failing to find a place for it in any of the other paintings, I suddenly decided it was worthy of one to itself – on a large scale too. I have not quite managed to capture all the shine and radiance but I feel I deserve A for Effort.

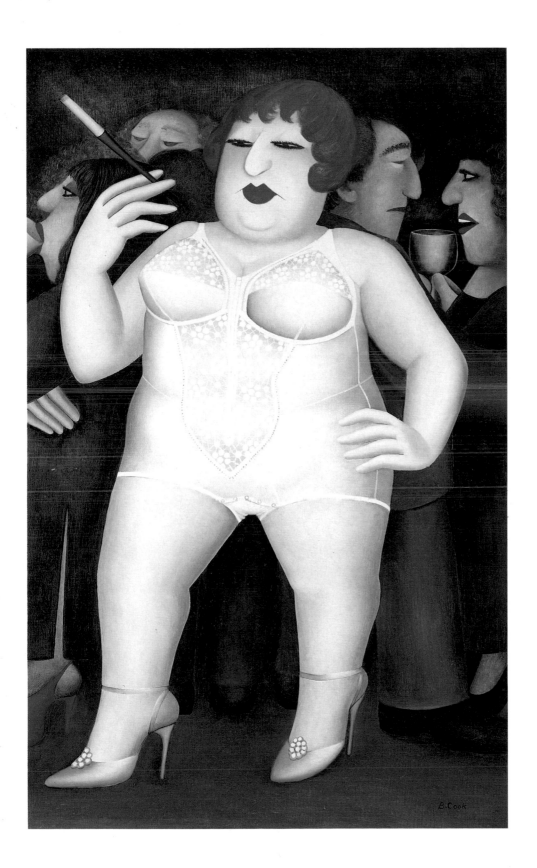

BUSTER

We left Albemarle Street and walked along Piccadilly to The Grapes in Shepherd Market for a much needed restorative. Buster, a tiny fat dog in a large jewelled collar appeared, followed by his owner and a friend. He was most appealing and quite accustomed to being petted and admired. But things suddenly turned ugly and he snarled and growled with all his teeth bared when the time came for his lead to be attached. Fortunately the friend found a chocolate (from Fortnum & Mason, I hope) and after a certain amount of wrestling all three trotted off. Soon after we did the same, to St James's Park.

BIRDS
IN ST JAMES'S PARK

We often have a rest in this park and sometimes walk through it early in the morning before starting the day's activities. There is not much park and a great deal of bird in this picture, and when it was finished I seriously wondered whether I'd ever paint another feather again. As my models were not entirely co-operative about standing together in a graceful group under a weeping willow, I made a lot of notes and then arranged them to my satisfaction when I got home.

STREET IN SOHO

I find it rather difficult to imagine myself in some of
the underwear I see in the shops in Soho although I
have tried to do so. We go past these on our way to
buy fruit from the stalls in Berwick Street market,
and lovely it looks too, all laid out for sale. Another
stop is the bookshop where I might find one of the
annuals I used to read as a child in the thirties. A big
mock raccoon coat kept me warm on the last visit so
I've given this to the blonde. The poor soul at the
front is meant to be an old lady I saw perched on
a stool beside her fruit stall, serenely watching
the passers-by.

BED SHOW

This one, seated invitingly in an open doorway, was
quite serene too. The night was young and business
was slow, but everything is ready for the rush.
Meanwhile, a quiet smoke and some philosophical
contemplation.

Madam Jo-Jo's

We had passed the Bed Show on our way to Madam
Jo-Jo's, a dear little theatre reached down a long
flight of stairs. We sat in the balcony and watched
the floorshow beneath us. To our great pleasure we
discovered that Brian, an old friend from Plymouth,
was appearing there. Here he is, dressed as a
bumble-bee and singing to some suitably attired
'flowers'.

RUBY VENEZUELA

The show was marvellous, such fun, and afterwards Brian asked if we would like to go to the Piano Bar where anyone who likes may sing a song at the piano. Some, I found from 'Beryl' (who comperes these concerts) may be allowed to sing longer than others, and there are just a few who will never be allowed to sing again after the first few bars! Here is Brian, dressed to kill in one of his Ruby Venezuela costumes, leading us up the stairs to get there.

BERMONDSEY MARKET

All the best deals are done here
before daylight in the winter, and
although we had breakfast at 6.30,
by the time we got to the market,
business had been brisk for an
hour or two. I'm addicted to junk,
I'm afraid, and will give a good
home to any number of cracked,
chipped and unnecessary items.
This of course involves further
purchases of cupboards and
cabinets to put them in, and I hope
it won't eventually mean the
purchase of a warehouse to
contain it all. Some of this junk
actually became useful at last and
has been carefully painted into this
picture. The ostrich egg is a great
favourite.

TEA
COFFEE
COKE
SOUP
CHIPS
SAUSAGE
TOAST

B.Cook

SMITHFIELD MARKET

Another early morning visit. Exciting too with all
the bustle and activity, great big sides of beef
manoeuvered into place and row upon row of
lambs' carcasses. Best of all were the dozens of
porters busily lifting and pushing, and I have
brought as many as possible into the picture. I
needed to consult our own butcher several times
when I came to painting the meat, and the fine large
sirloin behind the shoulder of the man with the
trolley is the one we enjoyed after it had served
as a model.

LUNCHTIME REFRESHMENT

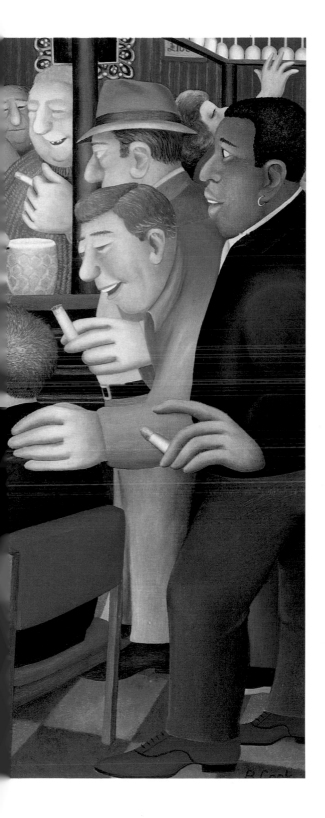

Down near the docks one morning we entered this nice old-fashioned pub, The Queen, for a well-earned drink, and a cheerful voice called out "Are you strippers?" The friend with us is in her eighties and I am a great-grandmother so in fits of giggles we settled down to a half-pint of beer and a doorstep sandwich each. To our surprise a lovely girl suddenly appeared and, dancing to music, peeled off most of her clothes. This was only a teaser, and a round of drinks later we had the full performance. What a bonus – and we'd only gone in to rest the feet for a half-hour or so. Refreshed, we left to continue our journey.

THE JAGUAR

The last time we went to the zoo, for the benefit of
our son who was then thirteen, he spent the whole
time throwing peanuts into the air for the pigeons to
catch, and completely ignored the animals. This
time, on our own, I was determined to see more of
them. After leaving the orang-utans, just inside the
entrance, our footsteps quickened rapidly to speed
us from cage to cage so as to shelter from the wind,
for it was a beastly cold day. The big cats, in their
beautiful coats, weren't bothered by the weather, or
us – safely behind a thick glass window. As I rather
like painting fur, and his is especially lustrous, I
decided to paint the jaguar, and set him against a
suitable wintry sky.

THE TIGER

After the jaguar I grew bolder, and thought I'd
tackle a tiger. And whilst I was at it I allowed him a
stroll through Kew Gardens, where we had been the
day before. So here he is, emerging from some
exotic foliage we found in the greenhouse there.

RIVERBOAT

We leave Kew to catch a boat back into London and this is the Queen Elizabeth, tiny riverboat sister to the QE2. Our sojourn on it was not long, alas. We arranged ourselves in good seats with a view, but as soon as it had filled up (to overflowing) we were told to get off as it had been booked for a private party. We were there long enough however for me to take some notes. I had been looking forward to the river trip, and it was a most comfortable boat with bar and refreshments which, fortunately, we had already sampled.

Tic-tac man

The day finished with a trip to Harringay Stadium, and in the picture things are hotting up for the next race. The tic-tac man is passing the odds (if that is the right expression) further on down the line. I had just made a bet so I hope I've put his fingers in the right position. I think I did, for a beautiful white dog called Leave Me Out won for me. If only I had been able to paint the dog herself! Despite many attempts I have been quite unable to get a picture of the dogs lined up together and, after the last failure, painted my winnings instead.

THE TOTE

And here are the winnings – well in fact they were £6.20 but I've increased
this to what I really hoped would be pushed towards me through the grill of
the tote, a nice fat wad of notes. There was a great deal of activity going on

behind the wire mesh, things were humming indeed, and after carefully
counting my small fortune I turned aside to do a little drawing.

THE SALES

A stay in London nearly always
involves a look in the shops, and the
sales will always tempt me in to find a
bargain. Many are the grave mistakes
I've made in getting one: discovering
this, in the privacy of the hotel
bedroom, there is then the additional
problem of finding an extra suitcase.
The method I now use is to attend the
sales, touch and try on to my heart's
content then put it all back on the
hangers and march smartly out of the
shop. This is most satisfying (and
economical).

Shoe shop

Shoes also receive minute attention from me, and I'm very interested in the changing styles. I regret the passing of the three-inch platform soles that were in vogue a few years ago. This style has come round twice in my lifetime, the first being forty years ago when I wore a pair to my wedding. Nowadays jumbo-sized plimsolls enable me to criss-cross continents in the utmost comfort. Excessively pointed, platform-soled, lizard-skin and louis-heeled shoes from the twenties are some that I've found in junk shops, and I keep catalogues of the new ones to use when I need to paint a pair in a picture.

THE CRITERION

Just a stagger away, after an exhausting bout of
shopping, is this cool and pleasant bar and
restaurant in Piccadilly Circus. Although I'm really
only interested in the figures in my paintings, and
always draw these first, I have tried here to show
part of the lovely art-nouveau decorations. The fluff
of greenery round the man's head disguises the fact
that I had some difficulty with the bar.

CAFÉ DE PARIS

Some very energetic dancing indeed goes on at tea-time in the Café de Paris, just a short walk from the Criterion. I have always enjoyed tea-dances – I admire the expertise and love the pretty dresses. One man told me he goes to a different dance every afternoon: no wonder he was so good, as indeed they all were. In my youth beans on toast used to be on the menu but I doubt if I could manage these now even if I could get them. This is the second tea-dancing picture I have painted and here I was fortunate in having a balcony and stairs to pack with people. Where I was unfortunate is that it was made of wrought iron......

Harrods

On our way to see a friend we passed this
enterprising man. He'd set up his wireless, put out
his hat, and was doing a nifty tap-dance outside an
entrance to Harrods. Very good it was, and
rewarding too, judged by the size of his collection. I
knew the ladies would need stylish outfits in
Knightsbridge and so have borrowed an ensemble
from Princess Diana for one of them.

SWEENEY'S

This is Denny, the friend who used to do my hair when we lived in Looe, in Cornwall. Now he has a smart salon in Beauchamp Place, and was wearing these attractive boots when we called to see him. These and the décor of the salon made up my mind to paint a picture. To complete it I've given him a customer with a great mass of ginger hair, much favoured by me.

JAZZ PUB

Arriving at Bertorelli's one evening for dinner and finding it closed, we turned into a nearby pub to discuss the next move. This didn't come until three hours later though, as a jazz band was in full swing, and made even more enjoyable by an elderly vocalist. I cannot remember having dinner at all that night, I only remember the band and the crowded pub. After I had managed to draw it all I couldn't resist adding the punk hairstyle that I'd seen recently – known as the 'Swordfish', my grand-daughter tells me.

Sultry afternoon

I think these two may have been to the underwear
shops in Soho. We found an ornate oval frame in
Bermondsey Market, and whilst lying on the bed in
the hotel one afternoon, I started to devise a picture

to fit it. Later that day I saw a girl in a pub lean
forward and place a cigarette in her friend's mouth,
and this little incident I added to the sketches
already made. Months later, after many struggles, I
finally managed to arrange it all to fit the frame.

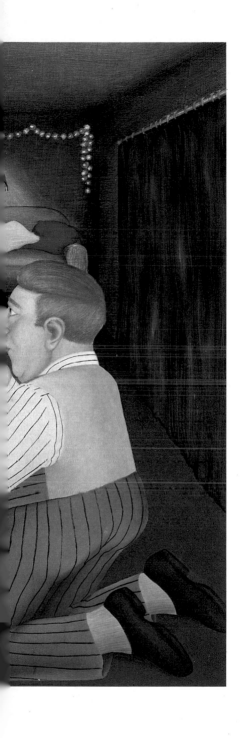

Personal services 1

I didn't attend this party but it must have been quite something! I had been following Madame Cyn's career with great interest and thoroughly enjoyed the book about her, so I was most pleased to be asked to paint two pictures for the film. In this one they are having a photograph taken at the start of frivolities.

PERSONAL SERVICES 2

And here is someone with a problem.

Dancing on the QE2

It is time to leave London now and sail away from
England on the QE2. Not for a rest though, for
every night is dancing night and all the pretty
dresses are out. These I thought were particularly
handsome. After I had painted the dresses I became
rather excited as they appeared to be moving about
in the picture, then I realised it was my eyes that
were dancing – from painting all those stripes.

Design by Ian Craig

Editor: Joe Whitlock Blundell

Beryl Cook's Paintings are sold in London
through Portal Gallery Ltd

Limited edition prints are available from The
Alexander Gallery, Bristol

Greetings cards and calendars are published by Gallery Five
Ltd, London

Original serigraphs and lithographs are
published by Flanagan Graphics Inc., Haverford, PA, USA